Dinosaur Museum

by Alice Maki

PEARSON

Scott
Foresman

Editorial Offices: Glenview, Illinois • Parsippany, New Jersey • New York, New York
Sales Offices: Needham, Massachusetts • Duluth, Georgia • Glenview, Illinois
Coppell, Texas • Sacramento, California • Mesa, Arizona

museum

Today we are at the museum.
A museum is a kind of building.
We will visit the dinosaurs.
Just follow the tracks.

tracks

plant eater

This dinosaur is very big. It is not real.
Real dinosaurs lived a long time ago.
The dinosaurs in the museum are robots.
Robots are machines.

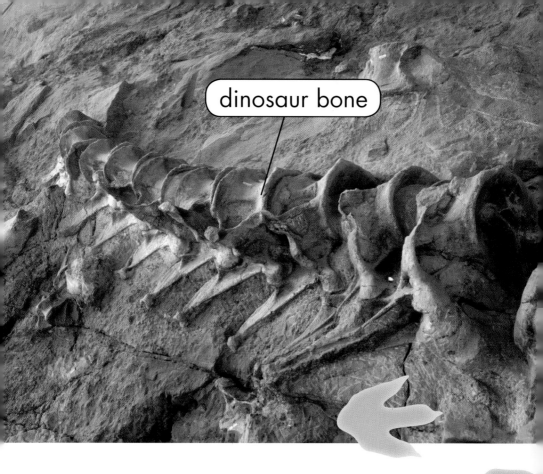

dinosaur bone

No person ever saw a live dinosaur. But we have found dinosaur bones. Dinosaur bones are clues. Clues help us know things. The clues about dinosaurs help people build dinosaur robots that seem real.

The clues don't answer all our questions.
Nobody knows what color dinosaurs
were. Nobody knows what sounds
they made.
Clues help scientists make a good guess.

plant eater

Dinosaur robots have iron bones and plastic skin. Each dinosaur robot has a computer inside. The computer makes the animal move and roar.

The robots seem real. They roar and move. They open their mouths. Some of the robots smell like dinosaur breath! Dinosaur breath does not smell good.

Museum visitors do not mind dinosaur breath. They like to see the dinosaurs. Would you like to get close to a dinosaur?